The *Unofficial* Harry Potter Joke and Riddle Book

D0018946

By

R. U. KIDDING M.E

Copyright © 2011 R. U. Kidding M.E
All rights reserved.

ISBN: 1466397675
ISBN 13: 9781466397675

Not by J. K. Rowling

Not Authorized

Not Categorized

Not Organized

Not Pasteurized

…but it's funny!!!

Chapter One: In the Classroom 1
Chapter Two: Dragon Breeding............................5
Chapter Three: Herbology 7
Chapter Four: Voldemort..................................... 11
Chapter Five: Azkaban Prison 15
Chapter Six: Around Hogwarts 17
Chapter Seven: Book List for Wizards 23
Chapter Eight: Off the Wall................................ 25
Chapter Nine: Knights 27
Chapter Ten: Fawkes the Phoenix...................... 29
Chapter Eleven: Norbert the Dragon 31
Chapter Twelve: Wizards..................................... 33
Chapter Thirteen: The Forbidden Forest 39
Chapter Fourteen: Vampires and Werewolves... 43
Chapter Fifteen: Goblins at Gringotts Bank..... 47
Chapter Sixteen: The Troll in the Bathroom.... 51
Chapter Seventeen: Witches 53
Chapter Eighteen: Ron and Hermione 55
Chapter Nineteen: Other Characters................. 61
Chapter Twenty: Harry... 63
Chapter Twenty One: J.K. Rowling 69

CHAPTER ONE

In the Classroom

Weasley: "Professor McGonagall, do you think that people should be punished for things they didn't do?"
Professor McGonagall: "No."
Weasley: "Well, I didn't do my homework."

Professor McGonagall: "In composition class, you brothers had exactly the same essay about your dog."
Fred & George: "We have the same dog!"

Professor McGonagall: "Niles, what happened in 1492?"
Niles: "I don't know, but there was a great party in 1526!"

Snape: "What can you tell me about *nitrates?*"
Niles: "They're cheaper than *day rates!*"

Snape: "Weasley, if you breathe oxygen in the day, what do you breathe at night?"
Weasley: "*Nitrogen!*"

Professor McGonagall: "How did they discover *iron ore?*"
Niles: "I heard they *smelt* it!"

Professor Moody: "How does Congress balance the budget?"
Hermione: "With *transfiguration!*"

Professor Dumbledore: "What spell do you use when you study anatomy?"
Harry: "*Abra cadaver!*"

Neville: "It's not that I don't like school, it's just the *principal* of the thing!"

Professor McGonagall: "Why is this paper blank?"
Neville: "I used disappearing ink!"

Snape: "What can you tell me about the wizards of the fourth century B.C.?
Weasley: "They're all dead!"

Professor McGonagall: "What's HCL?"
Harry: "It's right on the tip of my tongue..."
Professor McGonagall: "Well, spit it out quick! It's hydrochloric acid!"

Snape: "Harry, this is the fifth time you lost points for Gryffindor this week. Do you have anything to say for yourself?"
Harry: "I'm sure glad it's Friday!"

Why did Snape say sad things to his strawberry potion?
To make it a blueberry potion.

Why did Malfoy get mad in potions lab?
He reached his boiling point.

What kind of music did they play in potions lab?
Heavy metal

What kind of *pH* solutions did they make in first-year potions lab?
Basic

CHAPTER TWO

Dragon Breeding

Snape: "What do you get when you cross an abalone and a crocodile?"
Weasley: "A *crock of baloney!*"

Professor McGonagall: "What do you get when you cross a kangaroo and a cow?"
Harry: "A *milkshake!*"

Professor Dumbledore: "What happens when you cross a chicken with a racing form?"
Ron: "You get an animal that *lays odds!*"

Madame Pomfrey: "What do you get when you cross a film critic and a hippogriff?"
Neville: "A *hypocrite*."

Professor Moody: "What happens when you cross Albert Einstein and a hippogriff?"
Fred: "A *bird brain*."

Professor McGonagall: "What do you get when you cross a tarantula and a ceramic maker?"
Niles: "A *harry potter!*"

Professor Dumbledore: "What do you get when you cross a chicken and an earthquake?"
Ron: "*Scrambled eggs!*"

Madam Hooch: "What do you get when you cross a Quaffle ball and a comedian?"
Harry: "A *goof-ball!*"

CHAPTER THREE

Herbology

Why doesn't anyone listen to mandrake plants?
They are *blooming* idiots!

How do you know Madame Pomfrey's real hair
color?
By her *roots!*

Why was Madame Pomfrey so judgmental?
She knew a *sap* when she saw one!

Who was Madame Pomfrey's great grandfather?
Leaf Erickson.

How did Madame Pomfrey teach at another school besides Hogwarts?
She had a *branch* office.

Why was Madame Pomfrey so judgmental?
She knew a bad *seed* when she saw one!

How did Madame Pomfrey cure people?
With *stem* cells.

What is Madame Pomfrey's favorite magazine?
Weeder's Digest.

Why is Madame Pomfrey a busybody?
She has *dirt* on everybody!

What is Professor Moody's favorite flower?
Iris.

What did the mandrake order when he went to the Three Broomsticks?
Root beer.

How did we know the elm tree was moving?
He packed his *trunk*.

Why does Madame Pomfrey listen to trees?
Each tree has its own *bark*.

What happened when the mandrake was exposed to radiation?
It became a nuclear *plant*.

CHAPTER FOUR

Voldemort

What is the capital of Maryland?
Voldemort?

What do you call a partially bald wizard who loses a little more hair each day?
Baldy-more!

Voldemort goes to a seafood restaurant and asks: "Do you serve *crabs* here?"
The waiter says "We serve anyone who sits down!"

Why did Voldemort like hockey?
There was always a *face-off*.

Why didn't Voldemort go to the singles party?
Because every body was taken!

Why can't you trust Quirrell?
He is *two-faced*!

Why didn't Voldemort tell Harry what he did?
He didn't have the *heart*.

What did Voldemort eat for lunch?
I scream sandwich.

Why did Lucius open a photographic studio?
He liked to frame people.

What's Voldemort's favorite video game?
Mortal Combat.

Why did all the glass break when Voldemort fought Dumbledore?
They were all in *pane*.

Why was Voldemort's ball of fire late?
It was *dragon* its feet.

Why did Voldemort break his Motown records?
He liked to split his soul.

Why did Voldemort go to Jenny Craig?
He needed a *shape-shifter*.

Where did Harry go to look for Voldemort's soul?
House of Blues.

What did Voldemort say when he pushed the preacher into the goblet of fire?
Holy smoke!

What kind of tea does Malfoy drink?
Black tea.

When Malfoy was little, instead of a teddy bear they gave him a voodoo doll.

What is Voldemort's favorite song?
"I'm Bad" by Michael Jackson.

CHAPTER FIVE

Azkaban Prison

What do you call someone in Azkaban who makes mint candy?
A De-mint-or.

What's a prisoner's least favorite food?
Lox.

What did the prisoner of Azkaban say to the warden when he ran into him?
"Pardon me."

What did the werewolf prisoner of Azkaban say to the warden when he ran into him?
"Pawdon me."

How does a prisoner of Azkaban communicate?
With a *cell* phone.

Why did the warden give the prisoner of Azkaban acne medication?
He didn't want him to *break out.*

How do you give a drink to someone in Azkaban prison?
You have them come to the *bar.*

Why don't prisoners of Azkaban get B.O.?
They always have the *Right Guard.*

CHAPTER SIX

Around Hogwarts

What entrance do dull students use at Hogwarts?
They use the *dumbbell* door!

Why were there artists at the entrance to Hogwarts?
It was the *draw* bridge.

Why are students at Hogwarts happy?
They have school *spirits*.

What happens when pigs play with frogs?
They get *Hogwarts*!

What do you call a secret room that is full of breath mints?
The *Chamber of Sucrets.*

What do they serve for dinner at Hogwarts?
Hungarian *ghoulash.*

Why doesn't anyone study art at Hogwarts?
Because you don't look at the pictures, the pictures look at you.

Why did they put the elephants in the moat?
They had their *trunks* on.

Why did Hogwarts close?
Not enough *prophets.*

What's Hogsmeade's most popular magazine?
The New Porker.

Where do you buy chocolate boxing gloves?
Honeydukes!

Where do you buy *vomit*-flavored candy?
Honeypukes.

What happened in the restricted part of the library?
Someone tried to *Filch* a book!

How did the half-lion, half-bird get into Hogwarts?
Through the *Gryffin-door*!

What do you call a wizard who squeezes olives?
An *Olive-hander*!

What's the difference between *Hagrid* and congress?
One is huge and slow and not very smart, and the other is *Hagrid!*

Why didn't the boot hold water?
It had a *pour* hole.

What's the difference between a bad Quidditch player and a politician?
One is an *awful quaffler* and the other is a *lawful waffler*.

Which Quidditch player works in the zoo?
The Keeper.

What's a good name for a Quidditch team at Hogwarts?
The Flying Sorcerers.

Why was Slytherin kicked out of the Quidditch match?
They used *foul* balls.

What do you call a blonde girl who is a tattletale?
A *Golden Snitch*!

Why do some Quidditch players play the drums?
They are *Beaters*.

What is the spell to fix a broken octopus?
Octopus reparum.

What does Hagrid call last year's charms?
Ex-spells.

How did the map know everyone's position?
They had *iPhones*.

What singer do baby wizards like?
Lady Gaga.

Why did the wizard go to Weight Watchers?
She wanted a *shape-shifter.*

What's a shape-shifter's favorite movie?
Transformers.

Why did the shape-shifter take the guitar?
He needed the *lute.*

What's the difference between the *Mirror of Erised* and Neville?
The *Mirror of Erised* is polished and Neville is not.

Two students from Slytherin fell out of an airplane. One had a raft and the other a beach chair. Who survived?
Who cares?

What did they say when Snape was hungry?
"Severus is ravenous."

When is a rat not a rat?
When it's Peter Pettigrew.

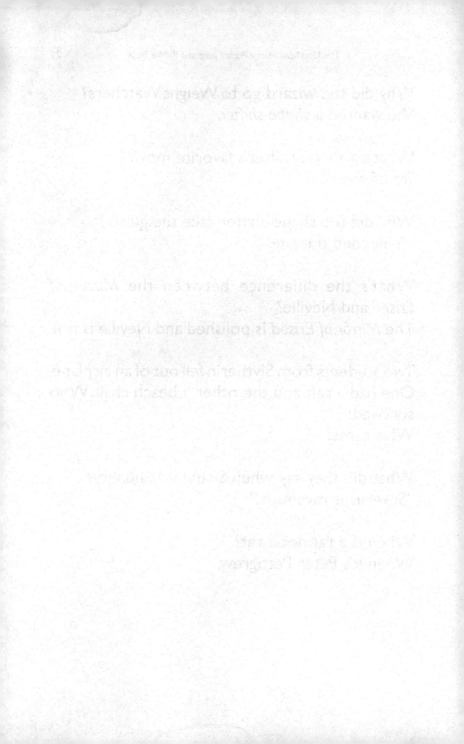

CHAPTER SEVEN

Book List for Wizards

How to Serve Humanity by Cannibal Tribe

Think Outside the Box by Zombies

If I Ran Hogwarts by Dr. Seuss

The Enema of the People by Ibsen

How to Fly a Broomstick by Orville and Wilbur Wrong

Transfiguration by Euclid

The Wizard of Gauze by Frank Embalm

Rebel Without His Claws by Olde Dragon

Goodnight Goon by Zombie Tribe

Alice in Wand a Land by Lewis Caroll

It's a Wand a Full Life by Knowe Waye

What's a goblin's favorite book?
Little Women

CHAPTER EIGHT

Off the Wall

What's on the wall of a skeleton's home?
Bone Sweet Bone.

What's on the wall of a Gringotts goblin's home?
Loans Sweet Loans.

What's on the wall of the Three Broomsticks Inn?
Scones Sweet Scones.

What's on the wall of the library at Hogwarts?
Tomes Sweet Tomes.

What's on the wall of the castle maker's house?
Stones Sweet Stones.

What's on the wall of the choir director's house?
Tones Sweet Tones.

What's on the wall of the Weasleys' garage?
Chrome Sweet Chrome.

CHAPTER NINE

Knights

Why couldn't Harry wear a suit of armor during the day?
Because it was a *knight*!

What kind of *spam* do knights eat?
Armour.

What did the knight eat for lunch?
Tuna *castle-roll*.

Why didn't the knight ask anyone to lend him a hand?
He had a *coat of arms*.

What did the knight name his son?
Lance.

Why did the wizard use *knight* labor?
It was cheaper than day labor.

Why did the knight lose the joust?
He was *horsing* around.

Why did the servant read the list of movies to the king?
He was the *title* page.

Why did the knight fight in the joust?
To test his *metal.*

Why did the knight have flat armor?
He sent his suit to the dry cleaners to be pressed.

CHAPTER TEN

Fawkes the Phoenix

Why can't you make a joke about a phoenix?
It always lays an egg!

Why didn't the phoenix kill the basilisk himself?
He was a *bird* brain.

Fawkes: "I want a cheeseburger with fries."
Waiter: "I have *The Order of the Phoenix*."

What's Fawkes's favorite soap?
Dove.

What do you call a phoenix that runs away?
A chicken.

What do you call a phoenix that can't fly?
A *Joaquin* Phoenix.

Why didn't Fawkes the phoenix lift the building?
Because then he would be a *crane*.

Why did Fawkes go to the polling booth?
He wanted to vote for *Quayle*.

What did Fawkes say when the hunter pointed
the gun at him?
"Duck!"

What did the phoenix say to the waiter about
the duck?
"He has the *bill*."

Why is Dumbledore's phoenix so smart?
He can out-*Fawkes* people.

CHAPTER ELEVEN

Norbert the Dragon

What's Norbert's favorite show?
Claw and Order.

How did Hagrid weigh Norbert?
By his *scales.*

Where did Hagrid go to get a new tail for Norbert?
A *re-tail* store.

What kind of cup does Norbert drink from?
A goblet of fire.

Why is Norbert a good boy scout?
He carries a campfire with him at all times.

What is Norbert's favorite rock group?
The Red Hot Chili Peppers.

What's Norbert's favorite song?
"Light My Fire."

Why did Harry like to listen to Norbert?
He had a *tail*.

What's Norbert's favorite seasoning?
Hot sauce.

What's Norbert's least favorite country?
Chile.

CHAPTER TWELVE

Wizards

How is General Motors like a wizard?
They took a *gremlin* and turned it into a lemon!

What's the difference between a dark wizard and
a bad economy?
One will attack you without being seen, sap you
of your energy, and frustrate you at every move,
and the other is a wizard!

If wizards are so smart, why do they always wear
dunce hats?

How do you buy a crystal ball?
They come in *quartz*.

How did the dyslexic wizard stop the curse?
He *dispelled* it.

What's a wizard's favorite rock group?
The *Wanderers*.

What type of tea do wizards in Los Angeles drink?
Pekoe and Sepulveda.

Why did the voodoo doctor go to the psychiatrist?
He needed a head shrinker.

Did you hear about the wizard who made a tea that turned Earl Gray?

Did you hear about the wizard who could make Oliver Twist?

In *Harry Potter and the Order of the Phoenix*, what are the Hogwarts students who got together after school to study called?
Nerds.

What's Dumbledore's favorite city?
Phoenix.

How do wizard rock bands defend themselves from evil?
They use *Brittney Spears.*

What's a wizard dentist's favorite movie?
Jaws.

Why did Dumbledore try to forget?
His memory was vial.

What did the wizard name his daughter?
Wanda.

What's a wizard's favorite movie?
Gone with the Wand.

What is the weakest part of a wooden wand?
The *sap* who holds it.

What do you call Dumbledore when he holds a goblet?
A cup and *sorcerer.*

Why did the wizard use organic shampoo?
He wanted to be *supernatural.*

Why did the wizard have mold-making equipment?
He wanted to cast a spell.

What does Dumbledore's mother say when she sees him?
"You need to get a shave and a haircut, and when are you going to get a real job?"

What did Mad-Eye Moody say when his glass eye rolled down the drain?
"I guess I lost another *pupil*!"

What kind of humor does Professor Moody like?
Vitreous humor.

What did Professor Moody say when Professor Dumbledore gave him an order?
"Aye, *Eye*, Professor!"

Why did Professor McGonagall wear high-top shoes?
So she could be *Puss 'n Boots*.

What did the Jewish wizard say?
"Watch me pull a *Rabbi* out of my hat!"

What did Nearly Headless Nick drink at lunch?
Evaporated milk.

Flamel is five hundred years old.
Why didn't they celebrate his birthday?
Not enough candles!

CHAPTER THIRTEEN

The Forbidden Forest

What should students do when they enter the Forbidden Forest?
Make like a tree and *leave*!

Why does the Forbidden Forest smell so bad?
Barking spiders.

What's the difference between a spider and a lawyer?

One is a low-level animal that waits for its prey and drains it of all its blood, and the other is a spider.

One day a lawyer went into the forbidden forest. An army of spiders surrounded him, but they didn't touch him. Why not?
Professional courtesy.

What's the elm tree's favorite rock group?
Twisted Sister.

What is a wasp's blood type?
Bee.

Why did all the post owls hang out together?
Mail bonding.

Why doesn't the basilisk wear glasses?
No optometrist can look it in the eye.

Did you hear about the snake that wrote a Hungarian rhapsody?
His name was *Franz Basil-Lisk.*

Why did the man get on the horse?
To make himself the *centaur* of attention.

Who has blood type 1/2 A?
The half-blood prince.

What do you call Hedwig the owl when she delivers mail at 2 a.m.?
The early bird.

What would you call a stuffed dog that went into the wash with lots of fabric softener and came out with three heads?
Fluffy.

Why is Fluffy so smart?
Because three heads are better than one!

Why was Harry sad when he didn't get any mail?
Because his post-owl didn't give a hoot!

One day, Fluffy was playing Bach on the piano and Malfoy was making fun of him. Every time Malfoy said something bad, Fluffy growled at him.
Hagrid said "Don't worry, Malfoy. His Bach is worse than his bite!"

How does the tree in the Forbidden Forest call Fluffy?
With its *bark*!

What did the unicorn say when she went to the doctor?
"I'm feeling a little *horse*."

What did the unicorn say when the other unicorn ran into him?
"Next time, honk your horn!"

What did the dragon say to the unicorn, after the unicorn told him his amazing ideas?
"You're not for real."

What did the unicorn say after he teased the dragon?
"Don't get mad, I was just *horsing* around."

Why did Hagrid think the unicorn was sad?
He had a long face.

Why are deer never hungry in the forbidden forest?
They always keep a little *doe* with them.

What's a basilisk's favorite subject?
Hisssstory.

What's a basilisk's favorite game?
Swallow the leader.

CHAPTER FOURTEEN

Vampires and Werewolves

What kind of fur do werewolves make in the potions lab?
Aldehyde.

Why did the vampire go to jail?
He tried to rob the *blood* bank.

What rank did the vampire get in the army?
Corpuscle.

Where does the vampire go potty?
In the *bat room*.

What is a vampire's least favorite food?
Stake.

What's a werewolf's favorite song?
"Blue Moon."

What's a werewolf's favorite book?
The Call of the Wild.

What do werewolves dream about at night?
Lassie.

What's a werewolf's favorite painting?
The Scream.

What's a werewolf's favorite food?
Scooby Snacks.

How did the vampire get anemia?
He kept attacking *half-bloods*.

Why don't werewolves attack *mudbloods*?
They taste terrible.

Why did the werewolf attack the beautiful girl?
She was *gore-juice.*

What's a werewolf's least favorite food?
Moon Pies.

Why do werewolves live in the forest?
They like *ruffing* it.

Why was the werewolf on top of the house?
He liked the *woof.*

Why do werewolves go to church?
To sing *Howl-elujah.*

Why did they foreclose on Neptune's house?
It was *underwater.*

What did one bone say to the other?
"Let's get out of this *joint!*"

What did the skeleton eat for lunch?
Ribs.

CHAPTER FIFTEEN

Goblins at Gringotts Bank

What do goblins say when they get married?
"It's better to love a short girl than never to love a tall!"

What happens when a wizard points his wand at a goblin?
The goblin gets the short end of the stick.

Why can't Malfoy go to Gringotts?
Because there's no *accounting* for him!

Hagrid: "Did anyone lose a large bunch of bills with a rubber band around it?"
Goblin: "I did."
Hagrid: "Well, I just found the rubber band!"

Why did Gringotts fire the goblin?
He came up *short*!

Why did the phoenix go to Gringotts?
To deposit his nest egg.

What do you call it when a vampire works with a Gringotts employee?
Batman and Goblin

What did the goblin say when Gringotts got robbed?
It's not my vault.

Why didn't Hogwarts school keep their account at Gringotts?
They had no *principal* (only a headmaster).

What kind of fish works at Gringotts?
A *loan shark*.

Why do rabbits work at Gringotts?
They are good at *multiplying*.

Why didn't the pretty girl keep her money at Gringotts?
She had no *interest* there.

CHAPTER SIXTEEN

The Troll in the Bathroom

How did Harry feel after the troll was killed in the girls' bathroom?
He was all *flushed*!

How did Hermione feel when the troll came into the bathroom?
She had a *sinking* feeling.

How did Hermione feel after the troll was killed?
She was *drained* of fear.

How would Harry and Ron get through the bathroom door when the troll was in there?
They could *faucet* open.

On what did they write the story about the troll in the bathroom?
Toilet paper.

Why did the troll join all the extracurricular activities at Hogwarts?
He liked *clubs*.

CHAPTER SEVENTEEN

Witches

Why are witches' houses so neat?
They always have a broomstick nearby.

What kind of broomstick do you ride in the rain?
A *nimbus* 2000.

What kind of broomstick do you ride in outer space?
A *comet* 260.

Why did the witch get a gun?
She was going on a *witch hunt*.

What's a witch's favorite book?
Cauldron of the Wild.

Why did the witch go to Starbucks?
She needed a better brew.

What did the witch name her baby?
Hazel.

Why did the witch take woodshop?
She liked *witchcraft.*

What do you call a witch at the beach?
A sand-*witch.*

What's it called when a wasp practices witchcraft?
*Bee-*witched.

CHAPTER EIGHTEEN

Ron and Hermione

Ron: "Kiss me!"
Hermione: "My lips are chapped."
Ron: "One more chap won't hurt them!"

Why did the newlyweds go to the Harry Potter movie?
They loved each *shudder*!

Hermione: "Would you die for me?"
Ron: "No, mine is an undying love."

Why did Ron take Hermione on a rocket?
He wanted their relationship to *take off!*

Why did Ron put on dark sunglasses when Hermione was near?
She was much *brighter* than he was.

Why did Ron and Hermione put their handprints together in front of *Mann's Chinese Theatre*?
They wanted to *cement* their relationship.

What fruit did Ron give to Hermione?
Her first real *date.*

What do you call Hermione after she fights sea monsters?
The *queen of the prawn.*

What do you call it when Ron and Hermione go tightrope walking together for three miles?
Going *steady.*

What did Ron say to Hermione when she showed Ron the way through the tunnel with her glowing wand?
"You Light Up My Life."

Why did Ron jump into the goblet of fire?
He wanted to be Hermione's *flame.*

What happened when Ron lost his broom?
Hermione gave him the *brush* off.

What is Ron's favorite food brand?
Banquet.

Who is Ron's favorite artist?
Munch.

Why did Scabbers get Ron in trouble?
Because he's a *rat!*

What happened when Hermione fixed Harry's glasses?
She made a *spectacle* of herself!

Snape: "What do you call the 'mirror' you look at, and in it you see yourself and all your fantasies?"
Hermione: "*Teen* magazine."

Why can't Ron use a computer?
Because he has a *rat* instead of a *mouse.*

What do you get if you trip and fall over Ron's pet rat?
Scabbers!

What do you call a rat that obeys the commands of other people?
Chuck E. Cheese.

Why does everyone hate Peter Pettigrew?
He's a *rat.*

How did Ron get immunized?
With *floo* powder.

What's Scabbers's favorite magazine?
My Squeakly Reader.

What is the most dangerous part of the Weasleys' flying car?
The *nut* behind the wheel.

Why didn't the Weasleys have a better car?
They couldn't a-*Ford* one.

What did Malfoy say when he crashed his father's car?
"That's the way the Mercedes-*Benz.*"

When Harry was in Ron's car, why didn't the door work like a door?
Because it was *ajar*.

CHAPTER NINETEEN

Other Characters

Why did Neville cast a spell to levitate his watch?
He wanted to see time fly!

Why did Neville make the margarine rise?
He wanted to see a *butterfly*!

Why did Neville fight the wrong ghost?
He made a *grave* mistake.

What do alligators eat for lunch?
Moat-loaf.

Why didn't Neville play cards?
He was the *joker*.

Why didn't Neville climb trees?
He was the *sap*.

How did Neville come up with a right answer in potions lab?
It just *crystallized*.

Why did Fred and George say they were twins?
They were *womb*-mates!

What did Fred say to George?
There is always *womb* for one more.

What kind of underwear did Fred and George wear before they were born?
Fruit of the Womb.

CHAPTER TWENTY

Harry

Student: "I see a scar on your forehead. Are you Harry Potter?"
Harry: "No, it's Halloween!"

Student: "How did you get that scar on your forehead?"
Harry: "Learning to eat with a fork!"

What kind of toothpaste does Harry Potter use?
Gryffindor *Crest!*

Why did Malfoy push Daniel Radcliffe off the Empire State Building?
He wanted him to be a *hit* on Broadway!

Why didn't Harry use a crystal ball?
He could save money by using *Sprint*!

Why did Harry take Triaminic?
To stop the *coffin!*

Why did the post office want Harry Potter?
He speaks *parcel*-tongue.

What did Harry write his essay on?
Parchment.

Why didn't the mummy help Harry when he was in trouble?
He was all tied up!

Why didn't the skeleton save Harry?
He didn't have any guts.

What did Harry potter say when he met his godfather?
"Are you *Sirius?*"

How did Harry get out from underwater?
He yelled for *kelp*.

How did Harry perform while underwater in the Triwizard Tournament?
He made a *splash!*

Why was Harry good at geometry?
He could handle *shape-shifters*.

Why did Harry go down the long staircase?
To see his *step*father.

Why did Harry have nightmares?
The horses were all taken.

Why did Harry run when the dragon roared?
He was in the line of fire.

Why didn't Harry listen to Malfoy play harp?
It was a *lyre*.

Why didn't Harry Potter brush his teeth?
He wanted to make a film.

How did Harry get into the chamber of soul?
He used Alicia Keyes.

How did Harry clean up a messy house?
He used *Three Broomsticks*.

How did Harry get more soul?
By using *iTunes*.

What do you call an old oven mitt?
A Harry *Potholder*.

What's black and white and red all over?
Harry potter in a tuxedo after killing a basilisk.

What do you call it when Tom Riddle tells a joke
about Spiderman?
Marvolo comics.

Why did Harry have so much trouble getting to
Riddle's tomb?
Other people were dying to get in there.

What do you call Harry Potter after he shaves
his head?
Harry Krishna.

What do you call Harry Potter when he's valiant?
Harry Trueman.

What do you call Harry Potter when he goes on a banana boat?
Harry Belafonte.

Why did the Potter Puppets act that way?
They did as they *felt.*

How did Voldemort annoy the Potter Puppet?
He pulled its string.

What did the Potter Puppet Pals say when they got a new watch?
"What's that ticking noise?"

What did Harry think of the underwater task in the Triwizard Tournament?
He knew that something was fishy about it.

What kind of gum did Harry chew when he was underwater?
Trident.

What kind of sandwich did Harry eat when he was underwater?
Peanut butter and jellyfish.

Why did Harry stay underwater so long?
He did it on *porpoise*.

What did Harry think of the final challenge in the
Triwizard Tournament?
He was a-*mazed* by it!

Why did Harry eat corn before the Triwizard
Tournament?
To get through the *maize*.

J. K. Rowling and Her Books

Why could J. K. Rowling have Harry write sentences again and again?
She had the *copyright!*

Why will Harry Potter last forever?
The stories will just keep on *Rowling* along.

What do you call J. K. Rowling after writing seven successful Harry Potter books and having eight movies made about him?
Rich!

Why did J. K. Rowling stop judging characters?
She was tired of typing.

Why does J. K. Rowling spell goblin like "goeblin"?
In Eengland they always put an extra *E* in words like goeblin and Roewling.

Why does J. K. Rowling live in a castle?
She likes to be surrounded by *pages*.

What does J. K. Rowling use to decorate her Venetian blinds?
Word for Windows.

Why did J. K. Rowling follow the spiders to the forbidden forest?
To find her *web*site.

Why didn't J. K. Rowling talk to the shape-shifter?
She didn't like his typeface.

What did J. K. Rowling say before she destroyed a character in her book?
Your pages are numbered.

Why did J. K. Rowling put all her best admirers under the table?
She needed to make a table of *contents*.

Why is J. K. Rowling so thin?
She uses a word processor instead of a food processor.

Why do the prisoners of Azkaban stay in prison so long?
J. K. Rowling is good at sentencing.

Did you hear that J. K. Rowling invented a new computerized wand?
It has its own *spell* checker!

Why can't the author of this book (aka R. U. Kidding) go to the forbidden forest?
The squirrels are collecting nuts for the winter.

This riddle book is so bad, it needs to be buried.
Where are you going to bury it?
In *Riddle's* tomb!

CPSIA information can be obtained
at www.ICGtesting.com
Printed in the USA
BVOW06s1325250117
474465BV00009B/45/P